# Moments Encountered

### By

### Joanne Sherry Mitchell

©2025 Joanne Sherry Mitchell. All rights reserved
Including the right to reproduce this book or
Portions thereof in any form whatsoever,
Without permission in writing from the publisher.
Printed in the United States of America.

## BOOKS BY JOANNE SHERRY MITCHELL

Moments
Moments And Then Some
Moments When Night Becomes Day
Moments Gentle Hints to Life
Moments Not Things
Moments No Replacement Found
Moments With Mrs. Melissa Sherry Smith 5th Grade Class
Moments Treasured
Momentos De Risa, Dolor y Amor
Moments As Milestones
Πολύτιμες Στιγμές
The Pain We Call Love
Moments Encountered

**Visit Author's website**

www.momentsbyjoanne.com

**You may email her at**

moments@momentsbyjoanne.com

## ACKNOWLEDGEMENTS

Front Cover Art by Betsy Perez, VBHS winner

Back Cover Art by Khaola Roman, VBHS winner

Cover design edits by Victor Morales, Art Director Professional Management, Inc.

With special thanks for their recurring assistance with my writing to Betty Smith and Marie Bartlett

A special recognition to:

# Vero Beach High School art students for their talented art as shown in their illustrations

Huy Binh Duong (Benny), *I Race To Win*, page 5

Ailiana Miller, *Animals*, page 11

Ola Anna Branka, *Soft*, page 15

Keaghan Konieczko, *Horoscope Three Years Later*, page 17

Keaghan Konieczko, *Save Something For Next Time*, page 19

Sophia Goodfellow, *Bugs Die*, page 21

Sebastian Garcia, *Rain*, page 23

Betsy Perez, *Ferral Cats*, page 25

Brennan Hickman, *Watermelon According To Dale*, page 29

Gwen Maresca, *The Girl In The Peanuts Comic Strip*, page 34

Tatum Bridges, *Jail*, page 38

Sadie Amacher, *Drum Major*, page 41

Noah Ferrel, *Fly Fishing*, page 43

Makaiah Mulligan, *Simple Okay*, page 47

Ella Rosa Kilman, *Time For Solace*, page 51

Ola Anna Branka, *My New Friend*, page 53

Axel Figueroa, *Meals*, page 57

# ILLUSTRATIONS

Ava Maria Pereira Sette, *You Are No Good*, page 61

Logan Beasley, *The Year Of First*, page 69

Kayla Cruze, *Whitewash*, page 75

Elizabeth Farnham, *Guard The Bird Feeder*, page 82

Lissette Asencio, *Thanksgiving*, page 88

Aubry Williams, *The Drink Of Knowledge*, page 94

Kayla Martinez, *This Is A Day I Like*, page 99

Khaola Roman, *The Battle Of The Clicker*, page 102

Bailey Hatley, *Pathway Covered With Weeds*, page 104

Sydney Whitmore, *Hearing Has Gotten So Bad*, page 107

Leo Swanigan, *Bending*, page 111

Brittany Ortega, *I Watch Birds*, page 119

Addison Ames, *Home For The Night*, page 122-123

Arianna Cruz, *The Tripper*, page 127

Sadie Amacher, *Taking A Nap Instead*, page 128

Avery Wolf, *The Voice*, page 135

*This book is dedicated*
*To*

## *Yoly Lopez*

Our journey together
cultivated contentment and success
beyond our wildest imagination.
Grateful for our time together
know I love you.

# CONTENTS

| | |
|---|---|
| I Want To be | page 1 |
| Mom Gave Me | page 2 |
| If I Could | page 3 |
| Arrive | page 4 |
| I Race To Win | page 5 |
| Wish | page 6 |
| One Thought | page 7 |
| Recurring Nightmare | page 8 |
| It is Hard to Accept | page 9 |
| Animals | page 10 |
| Saturday Breakfast | page 12 |
| Talking | page 13 |
| Soft | page 14 |
| Horoscope Three Years Later | page 16 |
| Save Something For Next Time | page 18 |
| Bugs Die | page 20 |
| Heart Beating | page 22 |
| Rain | page 23 |
| Ferral Cats | page 24 |
| Fifth Day | page 26 |
| Gym | page 27 |
| Watermelon According To Dale | page 28 |
| Quirkiness | page 30 |
| Mom | page 31 |
| People's Birthday | page 32 |
| The Girl In The Peanuts Comic Strip | page 35 |
| Went to the Bathroom with Buzzing Flies, Bees and Mosquitos | page 36 |
| Jail | page 38 |
| Favorites | page 39 |
| Drum Major | page 40 |
| Fly Fishing | page 42 |
| Simple Okay | page 45 |
| If She Was My Wife, I'd Kill Her | page 48 |
| Street Of Stranges | page 49 |
| Time For Solace | page 50 |

| | |
|---|---|
| My New Friend | page 52 |
| Want Therapy | page 55 |
| Wanted | page 56 |
| Meals | page 57 |
| Safe Place | page 58 |
| Homework | page 60 |
| You Are No Good | page 61 |
| Pity | page 62 |
| Everyone Lies | page 64 |
| I Want | page 66 |
| The Thought | page 67 |
| The Year Of First | page 68 |
| Be Wise | page 70 |
| There Is A Fire | page 72 |
| Are You Available | page 73 |
| Whitewash | page 74 |
| Defying Reason | page 76 |
| Walking On By | page 77 |
| Why | page 78 |
| More Photos, Food, Drinks, Toast, Dances | page 79 |
| Mom | page 80 |
| Reconsider | page 81 |
| Guard The Bird Feeder | page 83 |
| Find The Best | page 84 |
| My Intention Was To Help | page 85 |
| Invited To A Wedding | page 86 |
| Full Moon And Love | page 87 |
| Thanksgiving | page 89 |
| Moonlight On A Lonely Night | page 90 |
| How Did The Name Happy New Year | page 91 |
| Why Can I Say What I Mean? | page 92 |
| The Drink Of Knowledge | page 95 |
| Smart Car | page 96 |
| What Happened | page 98 |
| This Is A Day I Like | page 99 |
| When You Do Not Know Them | page 100 |
| The Battle Of The Clicker | page 103 |

| | |
|---|---|
| Pathway Covered With Weeds | page 105 |
| My Life Has A Dividing Line | page 106 |
| Hearing Has Gotten So Bad | page 107 |
| Bathroom Stall | page 108 |
| Bending | page 110 |
| Night So Hard | page 112 |
| AI | page 113 |
| When I Graduated From High School | page 114 |
| Dad Had Trouble Hearing | page 116 |
| Strange | page 117 |
| I Watch Birds | page 118 |
| I am Fourteen | page 120 |
| Home For The Night | page 122 |
| Wanting My Journey | page 124 |
| Eternity | page 125 |
| The Tripper | page 126 |
| Taking A Nap Instead | page 128 |
| There Is A Book | page 130 |
| Stages | page 131 |
| Maryann Had The Biggest Breast I Have Ever Seen | page 132 |
| The Voice | page 134 |

## I WANT TO BE

Creative

Confident

Courageous

Compassionate

Celebrate life

Now that I know

What I want

I am on my way

## MOM GAVE ME

Everything I asked for

That is what I feel

Even though I am

Sure, she did not.

Yet

Every gift was something I loved

Always wrapped perfectly,

She took the time for me.

I gave her a plastic pair of earrings

I made in junior high

I found those earrings

In her jewelry box

After she was gone,

I often think of that

Moment of discovery.

Mom

Did I give you enough?

**IF I COULD**

I would want to hear

Our song each day.

I can promise

Each time I hear

Our song

Brings me

Back, to the

Beginning

When all was

Right.

Clearing my

Calendar

For our

Tomorrow.

## ARRIVE

That is the point

To arrive

In one piece.

Forget speed or

Yelling at poor drivers

Keep in mind

They cannot hear you.

Your emotions will

Spin you out of control

Leave a bit early

No rushing

Rushing will buy you one

Maybe two minutes

Position yourself to

Arrive in one piece.

**I RACE TO WIN**

I never ran a race

With the desire to

Come in second.

Huy Binh Duong (Benny)

## WISH

For a late winter

Long, dark days

Cold nights

Cold mornings.

Flowerless season of winter

We all could wait

A few weeks

To get winter started.


Autumn full of

Oranges, reds, and muted yellows

Butterflies and bees for filling

Their critical roles.

Autumn

Before the time when

Birds take flight

All the leaves fall

The joy of lingering

Autumn.

**ONE THOUGHT**

To always keep

Close to your heart

We all can do a

Little

To make a difference

Help is help;

Always needed

Take time.

**RECURRING NIGHMARE**

Circles around

At leisure,

To provide terror that will awaken you

In the middle of the night.

## IT IS HARD TO ACCEPT

When I first saw you

My love began,

Not wanting to end

Not wanting to share

There was no pleasing,

Your love has yet to start.

When I hear songs

With girlfriends' names

I stop the music

Turn the dial.

Try to heal my heart

Of the love that started

At first sight

Never, to be returned.

## ANIMALS

Smart

They run

Protect

Hide

Lay still,

When danger

Comes their way.

Even the tiniest

Of life

Goes in the opposite direction

When danger

Comes their way;

Follow their lead.

Ailiana Miller

## SATURDAY BREAKFAST

Thirty-six years of

Saturday breakfast

A tradition of sorts

The sisters

The continuity of our time together

The bonding of us.

Even if we miss a few Saturdays

When we return

We start just where we left off

Breakfast served

With memories

Of childhood

Motherhood

Marriage

Filled with tears, laughs, anticipation

Long time enjoyment

The connection that flows

Always in present time.

**TALKING**

With my granddaughter

"Yiayia"

She asks,

How many more sleeps

Before I come to visit?

Splendid,

She wants to come back.

## SOFT

Rains of Spring

Inspire

Each bloom

We know

Will arrive

With pleasure

For our hearts.


Soft

Rains of Spring

Gives us time

Listening to

Maidens' laughter

Anticipating

The capture of love.

Ola Anna Branca

Soft
Rains of Spring
Gives
The red cardinal
Understanding
Winter is over
Singing his song
As an old friend
Returns home.

## HOROSCOPE THREE YEARS LATER

To the date

Wednesday, September 18th, 2019

I found the newspaper tucked away

In my pajama drawer.

I picked up the paper

Thinking I saved this for a reason

Four pages folded, as

I do when riding the packed subway

Not to hit the passenger next to me

With the newspaper.

Not much in the news

I do notice the prices have gone up

This paper must have been saved for

The horoscope which reads

*Changes I make will benefit*

*Me and those that are important to me.*

Maybe this paper is tucked away

To remind me

Changes I make affect

Those that I love

I refold the paper
As a reminder
What I do affects loved ones.
The pajama drawer keeps my horoscope
Close and safe.

Keaghan Konieczko

## SAVE SOMETHING FOR NEXT TIME

Jim always says that
When we first started to take
Vacations
We tried to cram in everything
Guidebook in-hand
We searched for sites
Recommended
From books, friends, TV shows.
We tried
Looking for the best
Ten things to see in each city
Then he came up with the phrase
Save something for the next time
As if for sure
We will be back.
The urgency left
We see what we can
Make sure we linger for a glass of wine
Dessert
A slow stroll down any street
In small towns, in big cities
Now, we travel with ease.
We develop moments of play
Spontaneous conversations
Knowing full well we will not see everything
While missing everything

We see, we meet, we eat

Maybe not the best in guidebooks

Yet we create the best of trips

Enjoyable, relaxing, memorable.

We will return

For we

Saved something for next time.

Keaghan Konieczko

## BUGS DIE

With my sincerest hope

Since

I do not like bugs

Especially the flying ones.

I like getting out the fly swatter

Which I use for any bug I do not want

Very effective

One strong hit

The bug is dead

I bought a few

To do the job.

The ones I have

Are arranged in a

Clay pot hanging on the wall

The fly swatter has pretty, bright flowers

Looking like a bouquet

On the side I see

Not the side that kills bugs

Yes, bugs unwanted.

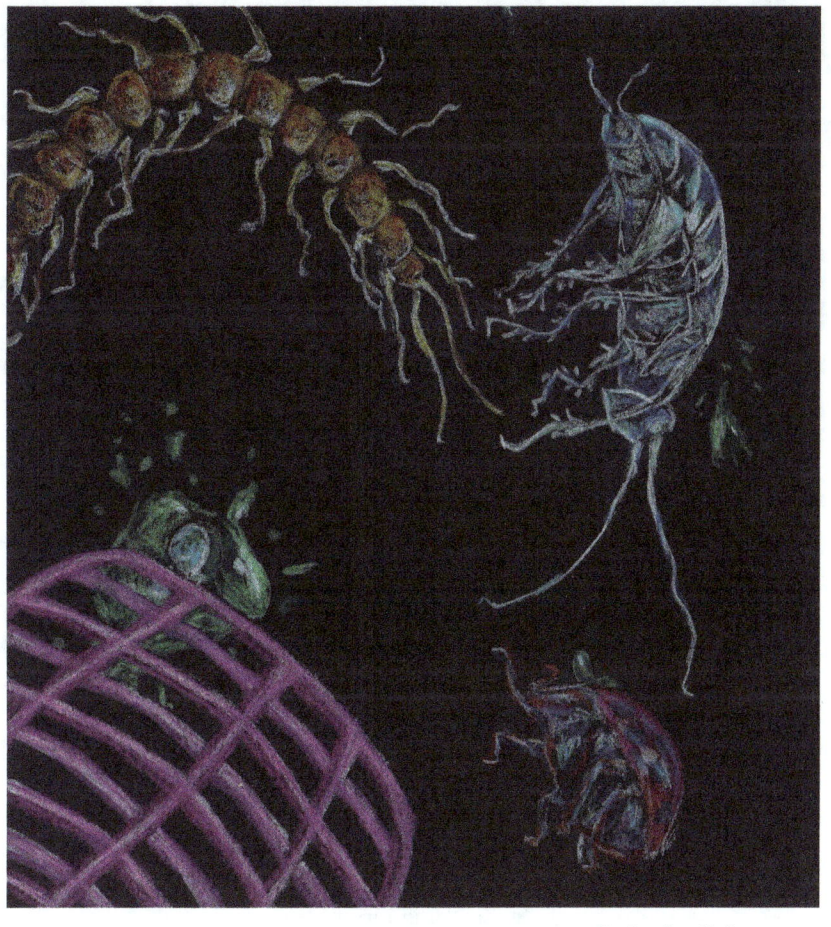

Sophia Goodfellow

## HEART BEATING

Exhilarating

With all the emotion

One's body could take

The way I felt

When first laid eyes on

My love

That's the beautiful

Edge of being a virgin

At nineteen.

You soar with the awakening of your body

Instincts debut

Changing your life's path.

What did it?

Who really knows

Frustrations mixed with desire

Alone in understanding, yet

Learning rapidly

The path love takes

As I begin war with self.

# RAIN

I can hear each drop

Fall

One at a time

Until thunder

Interrupts

Sebastian Garcia

## FERAL CATS

BB short for Black Bastard

My third feral cat

Each day BB and I are

Leaving the world for a short

Moment in time.

He brings me simplicity in comfort

More than

Anyone or anything I know.

He is peaceful

Never any mention of pain or disappointment

He expects to be called for meals

For which he puts on a methodical show

With his stretching

Arching his back

Rubbing up against my leg

Rolling over for a belly rub.

Wanting with BB

This slow-moving morning

Before hectic starts.

Betsy Perez

**FIFTH DAY**

On my diet

Have not lost

A single pound.

Doing something

Wrong

That is why, it's my

Ninth diet.

### **GYM**

I go and try

To exercise

Conversations

Get in the way, and

The best

Snacks in

The snack machine

Also get in the way

With more

Conversations

By then

It is time to go home.

## WATERMELON ACCORDING TO DALE

Dale helped us pick out a watermelon

"This is the best watermelon Georgia produces

Eat it cold

In the sunshine

On a perfect mountain day."

Today is that day

On our back porch

At our round black table

We sat

In our thirsty state

Devoured our watermelon

Letting the juices drip

Down our cheeks.

As our thirst was quenched in

The cool crisp air

Each of us remembering

How special watermelon can be.

Brennan Hickman

**QUIRKINESS**

When I was a kid
I knew ahead of time
I was doing wrong
Yet, I did it anyway.
I still do things
That will disappoint
A bit of agony appears
Within.
This nonsense
Must stop
Not a kid any longer.

## MOM

Simple I like writing about her
She did so much for me
She would stay up all night
Helping me with a project
Even though I fell
Asleep while she finished.
Now cancer takes all her time and energy
She does very little for me now
For Mom can no longer
Love through doing.
Now instead of doing for me
Mom mustards up the energy, to hug me
Tells me she loves me.
At times she adds little
Words that give so much
Like last night
Mom said, I love you
From the first moment I held you.
Felt good to know
How blessed I have been
I was loved my entire life.

## PEOPLE'S BIRTHDAYS

What do you want

I have asked the question often

When it comes to gift time

For loved ones

I think I know what they may like

Yet I do not.

Then I question myself, if you really knew them

You would know what to get.


When do you stop giving a birthday gift

At age forty-seven? I am thinking

By then, they should have everything

They want

Or they're able to live without.

Possibility

When they do not write you a thank you note

Good time to stop the gift giving.

I have a new practice

No way to forget anyone's birthday,

In January

Everyone I know

That I want to gift

Gets a birthday card

On the envelope I write

*Open on your birthday*

This way the wish is not late

Loved ones remembered.

As for the gift, it is money

With a cut-out of two or three items

They can buy with the money

This way they know I know them

A bit.

Gwen Maresca

## THE GIRL IN THE PEANUTS COMIC STRIP

Peddled her advice

On a homemade stand

As if she was selling lemonade.

I walked down my street

I wished the stand was here

When I need advice

There is no appointment needed

Close to home

Sidewalk advice by a little girl.

My question I would ask

I longed to become a teacher

Dad is so proud of me

Today I desire a better profession

With much more pay.

Can this girl in the makeshift stand

Tell me, it is ok

To let my dad down

Go for something I may like better.

Advice is needed if only for five cents.

## WENT TO THE BATHROOM WITH BUZZING FLIES, BEES, AND MOSQUITOS

First of all, people have to go to the bathroom

Anywhere anytime

If you're going to have bathrooms

They should be cleaned

Or hang a sign

*Bathrooms Dirty - Very Dirty*

Instead, we encountered the Park's bathroom

Expecting two useable bathrooms

One for men, one for women

We went to our rightful bathroom

We came out fast

It was filled with

Flies, bugs of all kinds

Did not stay long enough for identification

My love said;

*"There I was*

*My penis being eaten*

*Not sure what to do*

*Watch my penis swell from bites*

*Not on the agenda*

*Ran out, will worry about peeing later"*

I never went in

Opened and shut the door as soon

As I realized the filth, the stink, the bugs.

Next stop

CVS for Neosporin.

# JAIL

First night

Room ten by twelve

Small window

Locked door

White toilet

Tiny metal sink

Alone

Quiet

Closing in on lonely.

Tatum Bridges

## FAVORITES

That was a joke for many years

Who was mom's favorite?

One year we all took a picture

With a big number one, by each person

Mom wanted all eight to participate

Some took it very seriously

I was one of them

I hated the competition

A game I would never win.

I told mom

Take me out of the race

The competition it too much for me

What a relief for me

For mom knew

Each one of us wanted to be

Number one

Contest on

For all eight

Less one.

**DRUM MAJOR**

Gallant

Band member

He marched down the field

Kicking high

Twirling the baton

Knees in-time with

*Sousa's Miracle March.*

Loved watching the dance in marches

Blew me away

Music blaring

Heartbeat as loud

Yet, I fell in love

With another

That did not dance at all

His smile, not like our

Drum major's smile

It was his lips for kissing

That did me in.

Sadie Amacher

**FLY FISHING**

Fishing in Alaska

That was a dream of mine

Outdoors

Quiet streams

Walking in a rhythm

Each step brings

A world of peace.

Alone

Leaving behind a world so

Different

Noise, commotions, hurriedness

On to the life of birds

Blooming flowers

Trees as background

I walked to streams

I might have been the only person

Noah Ferrel

<blockquote>
Ever to see this spot.

At least, for this particular morning

I really do not want to catch a fish

It is the place

Giving me a sense of the
</blockquote>

*(continued)*

Power of quiet

The contentment of lingering.

I cast for hours

The rhythm is better than a dance

Of love

The smell of freshness

Encourages gratitude

That gives me strength

To go back home.

## SIMPLE OKAY

He called, asked if I was doing

Anything this Thursday afternoon

Even if I were busy

For this young man

I would, and did drop everything anytime he called.

He asked if we could meet in Coconut Grove

At the park on the bay

Great place to meet on the spare of the moment.

I asked Dad if I could have the car for an hour

Nothing we did took an hour

Dad said yes.

I loved his car, a vintage 58 Lincoln convertible

Of course, I put the top down

Drove at a speed over the limit.

We meet

He smiles, I smile

Just looking at him has me tipsy

We talk, hold hands

*(continued)*

He carves our initials, enclosed in a heart

On a palm tree.

I bought a snack, he bought a blanket

We ate the snack of oatmeal cookies, cold milk

We talked of nothing I remember

The feeling, the excitement, the comfort

Is what was remembered.

It was getting late; I had to bring back the car

We finally kissed, a goodbye kiss.

I got in the car, we kissed again

I drove off, excitement uncontrollable

As I turn to leave, I hit

Seven or eight poles with the car

That were in my way.

He laughed, I laughed

Hope your dad doesn't get too mad,

I race home

Dad thought it was funny too

He liked Jim.

The icing on the cake

Sunday's paper, I appeared in Jim Dooley's column

Who is that young good-looking girl

In the vintage Lincoln convertible

Racing down 19th Avenue?

Makaiah Mulligan

## IF SHE WAS MY WIFE, I'D KILL HER

This is Tony being angry with a fellow member
During a homeowner's association meeting

This woman talks and talks and talks
If it is not going her way

She will fight, to get her point across
To the entire board.

When it comes to vote she wants
Consensus

Even if her item passes by majority
She starts the grilling to change the vote

When she is at a meeting
We avoid items to vote on

At the end of the annual meeting
The most mild-mannered man I know

Tells me, "If that woman was my wife
I'd kill her".

## STREET OF STRANGERS

Yet the street is no stranger to me

We keep each other company.

When I long for food, he lets

Me beg for money while he holds me.

When I am so tired, I cannot walk another

Step nor beg for one more dime

He lets me lay down and rest

Most of the time, it is a very deep sleep

While I dream the freshness of dreams

For a better time to come.

You may think this is sad and

Very hard on me

It is not

For where I came from it is far worst.

## **TIME FOR SOLACE**

The walk I do each morning

Early as the sunrise

This walk

Does so much for me

Reduces stress when

The stress of life brings me turmoil

The needed exercise

The time to plan the day

The bonus, no one

Calls you before dawn

Nor is there a doctor's appointment

Or a teacher-parent conference.

The activity is easy on my body

Easy on my mind

Strange how there is no thinking about

How to walk or where

My feet always get me back home

One step at a time.

Ella Rose Kilman

## MY NEW FRIEND

I derive comfort from my new friend

When things stress me out

Pull out my iPhone

Play a game

I become absorbed

In the game

Forgetting what had stressed me out.

Before I fall asleep at night

I take my iPhone out, look at pictures

From days gone by

Most, if not all my pictures

Tell me of a time when I was happy

These great phones even

Put all the photos together, just by asking

I want all the pictures of this person

They identify just what I want

In a minute, I have all the photos of my grandson

This is from thousands of photos.

I can read a book

Watch a movie

I can invest

Pay bills

Do banking

My new friend keeps track of my steps

My heart rate, notifies me when it accelerates     *(continued)*

I can have deliveries to my door step

All sorts of foods, clothes, shoes.

iPhone, anywhere in the world

Can answer any questions asked

See the weather anywhere

Around the world or the next town over.

Any item I need fixed

It is on this new friend

With detailed directions

My toilet was running, running, and running

No plumber could come for three days

My iPhone showed me what I needed to do

What equipment was needed.

This goes on, anytime and everywhere

My friend the iPhone shops with me

Reads with me

Walks with me

Never complaints

Only issue I ever have is

When it is not charged.

## WANT THERAPY

Someone just to listen

To the kind of life, I have liked.

I want to give the therapist

The power to say

Good life

Your life not so good

You are one in a million

Not sure how you got through it all

No one was hurt by your actions

Your actions made one, a better person.

I want the report card

To sign the report card

Maybe mom and dad will sign

My report card

My dad would be happy, if I

Came out average

My mom would have wanted

One hundred percent.

I am compelled

To try therapy

Yielding my power to someone's opinion

A therapist.

**WANTED**

The love

That takes hold of my fear

In the middle of a storm

Soothes the anxiety

Prevents my heart from freezing

Until the storm has passed

## MEALS

Bring on sounds

The banging pots

The clanging of dishes

Opening of packages

The laughter at the dinner table

Conversations of family matters

The sounds that surround meals

At home

Axel Figueroa

## SAFE PLACE

We all need one

Even if it is a favorite bench

At the mall

Where no one knows you

You watch those that walk by

Soon you are focused on your dreams

Your desires

A bit of your past

How your kids are doing

How can you help your parents.

Time to take accounting of you

Think of it as a tax return

Every year we must collect

All the year's data.

Encounter and success

Organize the year

To know yourself

A bit better.

Find a sense of who

You

Have been this year

The self that grows dreams

Commits to helping others

Visiting relatives

Books you have read

The vacations you took

The vacations you did not take

What brought you joy

The sad times you overcame

Enlightened thoughts

Making your life less toxic.

Review if you will

The year

In your

Safe place.

## HOMEWORK

I now work from home

It is great in so many ways

I do not have to fight traffic

I do not have to get dressed

I can go to the bathroom whenever I want

I can make breakfast

Not eat on the run.

My puppy dog loves

To just sit at my feet, and listen

Watch and enjoy the

Warmth of our relationship.

The issue

I am now the boss of self

I must look in the mirror

Remind the person I see

It is time to get to work

Now.

## YOU ARE NO GOOD

You step on my heart

As if it is a roach

Watch the roach scurry

Before the heavy

Crushing foot puts out one's light

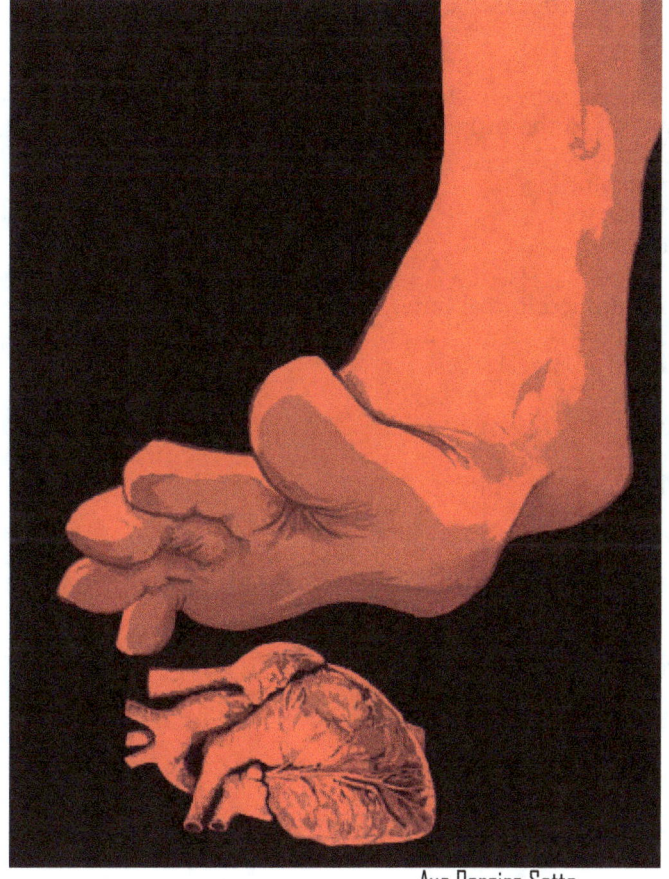

Ava Pereira Sette

**PITY**

When I was a kid

Pity for my grandsons

Most nights

We watched TV as a family.

We would sit around

Tune in to the program

No rewinding

No replay

We watched in real time.

After the *Perry Mason* or

*Father Knows Best* was over

We talked about it

We fought over what to watch next

We had to work it out, seven kids

One TV, one program at a time.

My grandson

At his home

Watches TV too

Watching in different rooms

For each room has a TV

His mom, even has a TV in her closet

Each member of the household

Can watch what he wants

When he wants

Alone.

There is rewinding

Surfing, one hundred choices

No fighting or discussion over what to watch

Unless, it is the internal fight

Done alone.

## EVERYONE LIES

That is the line I have heard

It is the line that I have read

Then, there is my sister

Who lies about everything and anything;

Her age

Her weight

Where she was born.

She is a widow, that lie

I find interesting

If she says she is divorced

They want to know why

How come

Are the children doing okay

What did he do wrong

More importantly

What did she do wrong.

As a widow there is nothing to be said

Except, I am so sorry

Can you see the difference?

We are at the park checking out

Pickle ball

We sit on the bench

Watch, start getting to know

The others that are watching

Ask each other, where we came from

It seems that everyone in this little town

Came from somewhere

I tell them New York.

Then, they ask about my sister

Where she came from

I tell them

You will have to ask her

She lies about everything.

Laughter by all

Then she says, Los Angeles

The liar at it again.

## I WANT

Summer

Year round

I need to drift

Take life slow

Enjoy birds at

My bird feeder

Take a nap

In the unoccupied hammock

Finish the books

I have started.

Dream of what I feel

How I lived my life

The loves

The failures

The successes.

Travel with the

Warmth of summer

Drifting.

**THE THOUGHT**

I harbor within

A memory

I never want to forget.

I have learned to

Close my eyes

Remember that kiss

On a rainy day.

We blocked out

The world

As we fogged up

The windows, of

The 1964

500 XL

Ford Galaxy.

## THE YEAR OF FIRST

1996

Learning to smoke

I had to practice first

I thought about

How to smoke and be a lady

The kind a man puts on a pedestal.

I sat in front of a mirror

Alone in my bedroom

I took out the cigarette

Put it to my mouth

Inhaled, exhaled

Still unlighted

I puffed gently

Then, with gusto

Held the cigarette in my left hand

In my right hand

Neither hand looked like

The cigarette belonged.

Then I decided to light-up

I watched in the mirror

Holding the match

Had to really inhale to get

The damn thing going.

Of course there was choking

Sneezing, coughing

This went on for at least an hour.

There was no way

I was going to be a

Smoker

Could not get the look of

The lady I want to be while

Smoking.

## BE WISE

Be healthy

Jimmy my grandson

Started all this.

He calls

Reads an article

He found

Explains how to be healthy

In a half-hour conversation/

While

My heart was busting with pride

This eight-year-old boy cares

About me

He starts with, you got to eat the right foods

He then proceeds to read off the list

Blueberries

Strawberries

Beans

Nuts

I listen quietly and

Acknowledge, yes for sure

I will watch what I eat.

Exercise is next Yiayia

It's a good thing you

Do so much,

No stopping your basketball and morning walks

I am so happy you take Papouli with you.

No smoking, no drugs

They are

Very harmful

Get some sleep too.

If you do this, you will

Live a long time

For I want you to be

Able to come to my graduation

For sure, I answer.

He loves me, he cares about me

And

I am going to Jimmy's

Graduation.

**THERE IS A FIRE**

That burns within

The fire of passion

It simmers

When not attended to

Grows in warmth

When attended to

## ARE YOU AVAILABLE

I want to spend time with you

Now,

I have it all planned.

We are going to start under the

Coconut palm trees

By the sea,

A gentle breeze

Go for a short walk.

The park, comes equipped with a pier

By the sea

Just made for people getting to know each other.

I will listen to you

If I like what you say

With a bit of comfort

I will call you back.

If I hear bitching of

Past loves or

What you do not have,

I promise

Not to call you

Ever again.

## WHITEWASH

Your action

Nothing else I could do

No telling why, you want me hurt

Leave it alone.

I think

You are too weak to destroy us completely

I am too weak to terminate us

No way am I going to let you go

Stupid me.

Bring on the whitewash

I will hide the dirt

Hide the hurt

Hide the loneliness

As I change the look.

Kayla Cruze

**DEFYING REASON**

That is what love does

You pretend everything is fine

You want this to go on

Never to end.

You put up with issues

You fear to address

You lie to your partner

More important, lie to yourself.

Understand where you want to stand

For

Issues with lies

Lose their importance

As you, lose your importance.

## WALKING ON BY

Oh my

Really you?

I thought it has been too long

I miss your laughter

I miss your dreams

I miss your optimism.

Help me mend my broken heart

And get back into

Your heart.

Missing the joy of you

So very simple

I want you back

The way it used to be

Any chance you have mending glue?

# WHY

Did he fall in love with me

Timing right

Dream date

The smell of attraction

Hopefully, I as a woman

Had hoped it was for beauty.

Dynamically diverse

The feel I give him when he touches

The ability to function in so many

Aspects of our life.

Yes, that is it

Good thought;

He chose me

For

Beauty

Abilities

Feel

Question no more.

## MORE PHOTOS, FOOD, DRINKS, TOAST, DANCES

The men go in one corner for the garter belt

For me and the other single girls

I hope I catch the bouquet, so I can take a photo

With the man that catches the garter.

As life is, I do get the photo

He is a cutie and a gentleman

He is seated in the chair waiting for the catcher of the bouquet

He gets up immediately for me to sit

"Thank you

Hi, I'm Betty"

"I'm Pete"

Maybe catching bouquet and garter belt, not silly after all.

This is for sure love at first sight

We giggle together

Smile for the photo

Hopefully when our kids ask

How did we meet

I can show them this moment.

## MOM

When you met dad

Were you pretty

*I am I hearing right*

Were you pretty?

I answer

*Dad will always think I am pretty*

*He loves me.*

My son answers

I am pretty too

You tell me you love me

All the time.

Glad he did not ask me if

I was sexy

Or

Did I have sex with dad

Before we were married.

Nah, he is only five

Pretty is for five-year-olds.

*Yes, I was pretty*

Should have been the answer

Without thinking.

## RECONSIDER

Saying

I love you

Save the term

For when and only when

There is truth in

Your

I love you

Elizabeth Farnham

## GUARD THE BIRD FEEDER

I wanted to watch the morning birds

With the seeds I place into the feeder

No such luck.

We have squirrels

That eat most of the seeds

Ducks eat what falls to the ground

The seeds that remain long after

Are growing into plants.

Birds are a no-show

While I watch uninvited guests

Invited by hunger.

**FIND THE BEST**

For your treasured heart

Choose wisely

With whomever

You give your heart

Then, work together

With love and kindness

## MY INTENTION WAS TO HELP

Could not work it out

My kids could not focus

I focused as if it were

Medicine to be taken.

Every single day

I worked until I had

Blisters, they slept late

I had the DNA that made

Focusing easy

The kids had the DNA that

Just used what I had.

Whatever I give them

Whatever I taught them

Was of little value.

They had to make a choice

The choice led to their

Destruction

My

Despair.

## INVITED TO A WEDDING

The lovely couple I have known
For six years, is making a comment
To each other
Now I must decide if I can go,
They're nudist.
The ceremony is taking place
Where all their nudist
Friends, acquaintances, and family gather.
Does a co-worker want to be seen
Without clothes?
I do not know about you
My body at this age
Looks far better with clothes on.
If I go
Do I pretend to be blind or
Wear dark sunglasses?
The wedding invitation
Should have stated; bride and groom
Will be in tux and gown
Guests come as you please.
I am going clothed
Why go naked when I want to look my best?

## FULL MOON AND LOVE

Love by the full moon

There is not a scene that excites me more

Than watching the full moon

Rise from the sea

Large enough to imagine it's a monster

Coming to visit.

We kiss until our lips are swollen

With a few mosquitos and their bites

When completed with our love secession

We watch the entire show given

To us by the

Full moon rise

We say our goodnights for

The night is over.

Now it is morning

I know

The full moon will rise again

In 29 and 1/4 days.

What I do not know

Will my girlfriend be mine in

29 and 1/4 days.

Lissette Asencio

## THANKSGIVING

The wishbone

Dries as we hibernate

Our tummies need to

Gain composure

Who gets elected to make the wish

A special wish

A wanted wish

A wish for health

A wish for wealth

No wasted wishes of evil.

When you snap the wishbone

Make sure everyone knows

To tell the wish

For it is not a secret

Wishes have a better chance of coming true

When shared.

## MOONLIGHT ON A LONELY NIGHT

Moon Goddess

Sparkles a plenty

Shines through the grand oak tree

Right into my window.

I lay in bed

Watching her rise

While she shines light

On my bed

Moon Goddess whispers to me

Why are you alone tonight?

There is no way to answer

The hurt of lonely

From the pit of my stomach

Which I held down with great skill.

Melancholy hits as I watch

The magic of nature

Wanting the

Magic of love

By moonlight.

## HOW DID THE NAME HAPPY NEW YEAR

Come into being?

We are trying to celebrate

An ending of a year

Welcoming a new one

Then someone came up with

The bright idea

Do a few resolutions

Why?

Each resolution says you need help

Getting yourself to perfect

Which eliminates

Happy New Year

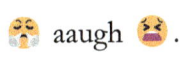 aaugh .

## WHY CAN'T I SAY WHAT I MEAN?

Yesterday my daughter told me
I have known him since I was fifteen
He was helping me with my herb garden
That is nice, is what I said.
But I wanted to say; you have not known him
Since you were fifteen
You may have met him fifteen years ago
You do not know him
You invited him to stay with you
For pleasure.

My next-door neighbor comes over
To show me pictures of her granddaughter
She is so cute
Is what I say.
What I wanted to say
What baby is not cute?

Can one picture be enough?
I do not want to see twenty-three pictures
Of your grandchild.

My son sits at the breakfast table
I ask
How was your night?
Okay, he says
Oh, that is nice.
I wanted to say
When are you going to be old enough
To tell me what you did last night?

I make no trouble
Keep others at ease
And
Talk within.

Aubry Williams

## THE DRINK OF KNOWLEDGE

Coffee

Make no mistake

Coffee, awakens my mind

As if it is a magic potion

Created by gods

Of yesterday.

They knew we needed

Help to start the day

With eyes partially shut

We sip the hot brewed coffee

Slowly, enjoying its warmth, mixed with

Smells that delight.

Awakened

Eyes wide opened

Brain begins its day's journey.

## SMART CAR

A bit too smart for me

I am into AI territory

Without permission from myself.

The car knows how often I use the sunroof

Maybe they should tell me

So I know, not to spend extra money

For the next car.

Doing a horrible job letting me know

All the information they store for themselves

Always leaving me out of the knowledge loop.

They know how often I charge my car

Where I charge my car

Even if I am due for a free charge

Which, they forget to tell me.

The car knows where I go

When I go

How many miles left, for a new charge

How far away I am from home.

My husband even knows

Where I am, all the time

Yes, all the time

Night and day

Seven days a week

Even holidays.

My husband does not even have to ask

What did you do today?

He knows before I come home.

All these advances making my head spin

Spinning faster than I learn

Navigating the complexities

Yet wanting to keep-up-to-date

With my incredible

Smart car.

## WHAT HAPPENED

I disagreed with your position

You got so mad at me

You stopped being my friend

It was about who I will vote for

Why not discuss?

Why not disagree with me?

Talk about it a bit

Why leave?

## THIS IS A DAY I LIKE

Fully rested

The weather, my friend today.

The sun is out bright

Temperature is spot on

Seventy-one degrees Fahrenheit

A breeze ever so slight

I walk to greet the day

Everything aligned.

Is this just for me, I ask?

Please let others see and feel the day

For it is like home

Welcoming my soul.

Kayla Martinez

## WHEN YOU DO NOT KNOW THEM

At a party

There are seven people

Sitting on a couch and two very

Cozy fluffy chairs.

I want to talk about

An article I read in The Times today

I wonder, should I?

What if they hate the idea of surgery

For underage transgenders?

I tell myself, think of something

Else to talk about

It's a matter of luck choosing the right conversation

It is the times we live in.

There is so much change and acceptance

Going on

People stand for what they believe

They all look normal

Diverse, engaging

Yet, I do not want to cause

Discomfort at a Saturday night party

We all came to have a bit of fun.

I cannot sit in silence,

I talk about the article

How it affected my life

I could not have the surgery.

Different times

The group said, how sorry they were

In different words and nods.

Nothing changed

Except, I did not keep

Silent this time.

Khaola Roman

## THE BATTLE OF THE CLICKER

I want to know what I am going to watch

My husband clicks

Fast, as his fingers can go

Never knowing what he watches

Not sure he wants to watch anything.

Click for variety

Click for exercise

He is not even looking for anything

He is looking for nothing

On the hunt

The joy of sport

On the road to

Nowhere.

Bailey Hatley

## PATHWAY COVERED WITH WEEDS

For travelers do not use this path

It is dark

Loaded with fallen leaves, and twigs from nature

Seldom used, for it is away from town.

Those that like their heart to tingle

Travel this path

For the straight path is no more.

Surprising, the meandering keeps one guessing

Bear right, bear left, straight ahead

Any, and all peril would be totally mine

I want to go alone

For it awakens the part of me that

Houses wanderlust.

Frightens those that do not travel in the woods

Thinking the path is loaded with surprise.

The power of this path gives me a sense of discovery

A path to learn the unfamiliar

About ourselves, and how we handle

What comes our way.

I just hope, it is not an

Unpredictable grizzly bear.

## MY LIFE HAS A DIVIDING LINE

The time before Mom and Dad got a divorce

The time after Mom and Dad got a divorce

The dividing line, when to step over

The dividing line, when not to step over

There was a dividing line for each parent

They hated each other

They wanted us to take sides.

I was so mad at both

Sides, had no validation

They were both wrong

They were both right

Bottom line, they thought we would get over

The divorce that changed our lives

We never did.

Our magic was gone

Parents wanted new good times

Sunday dinners, full of laughs and conversations were gone

Fighting over money began

The dividing line drawn among all of us.

While we hate what happened

After the divorce

We all found our way

To tip-toe around the dividing line.

## HEARING HAS GOTTEN SO BAD

Nine out of ten times he does not hear what I say

Worse, I feel he does not care to know what I say

Even worse, I am tired of talking.

We sit quietly on the sofa

Holding hands, once in a while

Works better than trying to hear each other.

Sydney Whitmore

## **BATHROOM STALL**

Hanging out here

I have been at the dance

For two hours

No one asked me to dance

No one offered to fetch me a drink

Bathroom stall welcomes

Me in my party dress.

Girls, I hear them

Coming and going

With the talk of

Did you see?

Did you know?

Please do not mention

The ugly girl by name

I want to remain

Innocent

Naïve

While waiting.

Not sure why

I hide out in

The bathroom

Boys never come

in

To ask me to dance

In a girls

Bathroom stall.

## BENDING

At the waist

Over my sleeping

Child

I was entrusted to

A lifetime of care.

Unsure how this will turn out

For

I want her to dance

In rainbows

In springtime, sun showers

Among the flowers that

Will bloom

In every color.

Nature's celebration

For a child.

Leo Swanigan

## NIGHT SO HARD

Long and lonely

Demons come

When the sun is gone

Little creatures

Big monsters

All come to scare me.

A young girl

Wanting sunshine

Not the long, scary cold night

I am so glad at sunrise

On time, each day

Rids me of demons, creatures, and

Monsters for a little while

That will visit

Again

In the middle of night.

## AI

It is the talk of the town

My imagination runs wild

When I think of all

The information

AI can store, retain, organize.

Gives back, in as many ways as

Your request

It is exciting and interactive

Inspires

Me to know more.

It is valuable

Compliments

My writing

I asked Chat GPT

To rephrase this

Passage

Chat GPT did so

Corrected all my spelling

Punctuation

Yet, I kept words as

Original.

## WHEN I GRADUATED FROM HIGH SCHOOL

I ranked 925 out of 1109 students

At the time I thought it was funny

As time passed, it began to set in

I was at the bottom of my class

I cannot allow that to be

Indicative of my entire life.

Somehow, I must be better

Move myself up in numbers

I cannot redo high school

I can only change what I do now.

I became competitive

In every endeavor

I had to outrank

Everyone I knew

In everything I did.

Always wanting people

To know I was good at

Tennis, basketball, chess

I had to be the best teacher,

Sell the most expensive homes.

Always in competition,

Wanting to give myself ranking

As if the millions and millions of

People really cared,

For sure they did not.

Today, I have stopped the stress

Of searching the best

Turns out, being competitive

Does not rank you.

I did just fine, better than most

Though not the best.

Looking back

925 turned out to be

A great ranking.

## DAD HAD TROUBLE HEARING

I did a mean thing

When I learned of

His poor, to no-hearing abilities.

I would yell

Dad

As loud as I could

To get his attention

Then, I would continue

Moving my lips

With nonsense

Just lip movements

No formation of words

And no sound.

Today, I want to say

Sorry dad

I confused you

When you needed

Understanding.

## STRANGE

I felt I lost

I was not even trying to win

Not even sure of the contest

I know, I did not enter one.

I hate competition

Unless it is with myself

Easy to win.

## I WATCH BIRDS

Building of their nest,

Does

Mother bird talk over with daddy bird?

What types of twigs to use?

How high in the tree will they build their nest?

Will they want a view?

Who decides how many eggs will reside

In the nest, they are busily building?

Do they confer with each other

Over every detail?

Always knowing

There is going to be one item overlooked

One item never thought of.

The tweets I hear, is their discussion

Wanting all to work out for their family

True voice of nature giving the best

For a family of blue birds.

Brittany Ortega

## I AM FOURTEEN

I want to drive a car on my own

At this time, it will be three years

May I add, three long years.

I know once I get my driver's license

I will have a bit of independence

Right now, everything I want

Or need I must ask my parents.

They hear almost every conversation

They know where I am each hour of the day

When I get my driver's license

I will be able to go to the store

Not only for me, but anyone in the family

That needs something

I will be able to do it for them.

I cannot tell you how many times

I hear mom or dad say

I am too tired to go to the store

I will go tomorrow on the way home from work.

When I get my driver's license

I can take my younger sister and her friend

To the park, instead of babysitting at home.

This driver's license will be a step

Closer to being an adult

Best of all, I can listen to my kind

Of music through

Bluetooth with the car's incredible speakers.

It is soon to be time to cut out my

Hovering parents

I know this will happen.

At fourteen, I dress myself, make breakfast on my own

I can even put in my own contact lenses

Just can't wait for the real independence

Driving to school.

# HOME FOR THE NIGHT

As I drive into my driveway

I see my cat sitting on the window sill

Quiet, listening, watching

As I approach, he continues to sit still.

I am going to copy the cat

Sit still for a while

Watch, listen quietly to our world.

Addison Ames

I think, how did I forget

The need to sit quietly

I find a place of beauty

To sit still.

There are so many sounds and sites

Birds at my bird feeder

Grasshopper soaking in the sun

Then, there is me

Quietly watching other living

Creatures, doing the same.

It really is uncomplicated

Copycatting contentment.

Addison Ames

## WANTING MY JOURNEY

Into love
To start
I want to know
What falling in love is all about

Starting the journey by reading
Famous love stories
Poems or songs

Get a handle on how people
Feel and think about love
It is a feeling, nothing to define

Catch it like a cold
Feel it, like a cool summer breeze
I am told, I will know when it comes

The journey that comes home
To your heart

I listen, look, and watch
Trying not to miss
What I want to catch

For my love
Will be the story worth telling
Allow me to belong

Not alone any longer
My very own monumental drama
Love will be worth the wait.

## ETERNITY

How will eternity look?

What is the path we take

To enter eternity?

There will be no answer

For no one, of all those

Who have gone to eternity

Revealed the mystery

Not even, my clever mom.

She swore that when

She entered eternity

She would figure out

The path back to me.

The secrets of eternity, yet to be revealed

Eleven years, seven days, give or

Take a few minutes

There has been no contact

Of our planned rendezvous with eternity.

Now it looks like

Mom will not get my hug

Until

In eternity.

## THE TRIPPER

Three days ago

I tripped at school

Right

In the lunchroom.

Not sure how it happened

It did, and

It still feels stupid

The metal lunch tray

Was so loud, everyone

Turned toward me

To see what happened

I had to get up off the floor

Pick up everything

The plastic dishes

The spilled food

Worse yet

My clothes, had food stains

All over them

All day long

In every class I went too.

Today, it is over

I have clean clothes on

I did not trip in the lunchroom.

I wonder, how long

I will worry about tripping

In the lunchroom

In front of the entire school

Worrying, about

What kids will think of me

The tripper.

Arianna Cruz

Sadie Amacher

## **TAKING A NAP INSTEAD**

He gets up to instruct four girls

They were trying out new croquet skills

He decided, he knew better

He was going to teach them

How to play the game

Instruct each shot.

*Girls listen*

*Try to comply with the directions*

He helps all four

At every shot.

Their game is over

Gone is the fun

Playing with laughter

Trails and misses

Girls' conversation

All gone.

Pressure on, with an uninvited teacher.

I got up and left

With their fun.

## THERE IS A BOOK

Written for all to read

Who is who

In this world of us

How does one get in

For I looked up my name and

I was not written about

Yet, I lived.

Who is who

Poking fun at all of us

Writing that there are those

Who have lived better

Suffered more

Laughed louder.

Time to be me, and

Bid farewell to the

Book of who is who

For I am.

## STAGES

When we first see each other
We went for each other
We needed each other
Could not wait for our first kiss

First night was the beginning of all our tomorrows
We knew angels planned our love
The magic happened

We were on the edge of everything possible
We knew our fortune was us
We loved dancing together

When we stopped dancing together
We did not need each other
Needless to kiss one more time
We ended with a whimper
Door slammed shut.

## MARYANN HAD THE BIGGEST BREASTS I HAVE EVER SEEN

We were only in tenth grade

My breasts had not started to

Develop,

While Maryann

Had the whole school talking.

Everyone

Wanted to know if they were for real

I knew they were for real,

I had Physical Ed with Maryann

That is when I felt the sorriest

For her.

We had to take showers

There she was

These huge breasts

Big as a melon, one for the right

One for the left

From her neck

To under her arms

Maryann's breasts covered

Her entire chest,

Trying to hide, while

Trying to stand tall

On the way to the shower.

At least

The girls

Could confirm that her breasts

Were real.

I know the boys wanted to see,

The girls prayed not to

Grow melons.

I stayed her friend

She stayed my friend

Flat-chested and the Melon-girl

Our nicknames.

## THE VOICE

Of the man opening

His front door

Going on his

Morning walk.

Asking with his

Inner voice

Wanting to know

Have I lived?

Avery Wolf

www.ingramcontent.com/pod-product-compliance
Lightning Source LLC
Chambersburg PA
CBHW050248010526
44107CB00003B/231